THE ULTIMATE
GREEN BAY PACKERS
TRIVIA BOOK

A Collection of Amazing Trivia Quizzes
and Fun Facts for Die-Hard Packers Fans!

Ray Walker

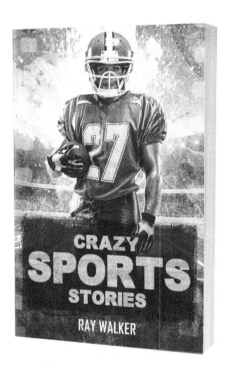

CONTENTS

Introduction...1

Chapter 1: Origins & History 3

    Quiz Time! 3

    Quiz Answers 8

    Did You Know? 9

Chapter 2: Jerseys & Numbers 12

    Quiz Time! 12

    Quiz Answers 17

    Did You Know? 18

Chapter 3: Packers Quarterbacks................................. 21

    Quiz Time! 21

    Quiz Answers 26

    Did You Know? 27

Chapter 4: The Pass Catchers....................................... 30

    Quiz Time! 30

    Quiz Answers 35

Did You Know?...36

Chapter 5: Running Wild..**39**

Quiz Time!...39

Quiz Answers..44

Did You Know?...45

Chapter 6: In the Trenches..**48**

Quiz Time!...48

Quiz Answers..54

Did You Know?...55

Chapter 7: The Back Seven..**58**

Quiz Time!...58

Quiz Answers..64

Did You Know?...65

Chapter 8: Odds & Ends & Awards...................................**68**

Quiz Time!...68

Quiz Answers..73

Did You Know?...74

Chapter 9: Nicknames **77**

Quiz Time!...77

Quiz Answers..82

Did You Know?...83

Chapter 10: Alma Maters **86**

    Quiz Time! 86

    Quiz Answers 91

    Did You Know? 92

Chapter 11: In the Draft Room **95**

    Quiz Time! 95

    Quiz Answers 101

    Did You Know? 102

Chapter 12: The Trading Post **105**

    Quiz Time! 105

    Quiz Answers 111

    Did You Know? 112

Chapter 13: Super Bowl Special **115**

    Quiz Time! 115

    Quiz Answers 121

    Did You Know? 122

Conclusion **125**

INTRODUCTION

The Green Bay Packers are one of the most beloved franchises in American professional sports. Their supporters are called "Cheeseheads," and they are among the most passionate and dedicated fans in the National Football League.

The Packers are the third-oldest franchise in professional football, and have a long and rich history of championship seasons and Hall of Fame players. The franchise has tasted both mediocrity and greatness, but has enjoyed unconditional support from its rabid fan base.

The mission of this book is to celebrate the football greats who helped the Packers win more NFL championships than any other league franchise. The list of legendary players and coaches is both vast and impressive. Team founder Curly Lambeau was the architect of the first Green Bay dynasty, and Vince Lombardi ushered in a new era of dominance.

This fact-laden trivia book includes a variety of multiple-choice questions that will test your knowledge of Packers history. Each chapter consists of interesting trivia questions that will challenge the most die-hard Packers fanatics.

Whether you are a novice cheesehead or a long-time Packers fan, this book will test your knowledge of the NFL's most decorated franchise.

The Packers are poised for another Super Bowl run in 2020, and top players like Aaron Rodgers, Davante Adams and Aaron Jones will undoubtedly put up eye-popping numbers once again. Whatever your purpose might be, use this book to learn more about your favorite NFL team and impress your family and friends at the same time.

CHAPTER 1:

ORIGINS & HISTORY

QUIZ TIME!

1. In which year was the Green Bay Packers football team founded?

   a. 1910

   b. 1913

   c. 1915

   d. 1919

2. The Green Bay Football Corporation was formed by local businessmen in 1922 to support the Packers financially.

   a. True

   b. False

3. What was the name of the company that sponsored the first team in Packers history?

   a. Rahr Brewery

   b. Dane County Title

   c. Indian Packing Co.

   d. Minhas Craft Brewery

4. In 1921, the franchise joined the American Professional Football Association. What was the official team name?

   a. Clair Packers
   b. Acme Packers
   c. MC Packers
   d. Rahr Packers

5. The Packers went 10-1 during the first season in 1919. Which team dealt the franchise their only loss?

   a. Madison Blues
   b. Racine Belles
   c. Eau Claire Tigers
   d. Beloit Fairies

6. Curly Lambeau and George Whitney Calhoun were the only two founders of the Packers franchise?

   a. True
   b. False

7. Who was elected the first team captain in Packers history?

   a. Al Petcka
   b. Curly Lambeau
   c. Dutch Dwyer
   d. Henry (Tubby) Bero

8. What was the name of the franchise before it was called the Packers?

   a. Green Bay Minks
   b. Green Bay Blizzard
   c. Green Bay Indians
   d. Green Bay Breweries

9. Who was the first official head coach in Packers history?

    a. Wes Leaper
    b. Jim Coffeen
    c. Gus Rosenow
    d. Willard Ryan

10. The Packers are the only publicly owned company with a board of directors in American professional sports.

    a. True
    b. False

11. Green Bay was booted from the league after the 1921 season for using three ineligible college players in a game. What college did the players attend?

    a. Illinois
    b. Michigan
    c. Penn State
    d. Notre Dame

12. What team did Curly Lambeau start coaching in 1950 after he resigned from the Packers?

    a. Dallas Texans
    b. Chicago Cardinals
    c. New York Giants
    d. Washington Redskins

13. Which of the following names has NOT been used by a Green Bay Packers cheerleading squad?

    a. Green Bay Cheer Team
    b. Green Bay Sideliners

c. Green Bay Packerettes

d. Green Bay Golden Girls

14. Only three current teams in the NFL, the Chicago Bears, the Arizona Cardinals and the Green Bay Packers are founding members.

a. True

b. False

15. What was the name of Lambeau Field when it first opened in 1957?

a. City Stadium II

b. Acme Stadium

c. Packer Stadium

d. Wisconsin Stadium

16. What is the nickname of historic Lambeau Field?

a. Title Park

b. The Frozen Tundra

c. Packers Park

d. Championship Stadium

17. Where is the Green Bay Packers Hall of Fame located?

a. Resch Center§

b. Lambeau Field

c. Weidner Center

d. Downtown Green Bay

18. The Packers established the first training facility in pro football history in 1946. What was the name of this training facility?

a. Wisconsin Place

b. Borchert Field

c. Bellevue Park

d. Rockwood Lodge

19. Green Bay was the second smallest city in the NFL when it joined in 1921 and, except for a short time in the mid to late 1920s, Green Bay has been the smallest city ever since.

a. True

b. False

20. Where did the Packers originally play their home games?

a. City Stadium

b. Borchert Field

c. Hagemeister Park

d. Marquette Stadium

QUIZ ANSWERS

1. D - 1919

2. A - True

3. C - Indian Packing Co.

4. B - Acme Packers

5. D - Beloit Fairies

6. A - True

7. B - Curly Lambeau

8. C - Green Bay Indians

9. D - Willard Ryan

10. A - True

11. D - Notre Dame

12. B - Chicago Cardinals

13. A - Green Bay Cheer Team

14. B - False

15. A - City Stadium

16. B - The Frozen Tundra

17. B - Lambeau Field

18. D - Rockwood Lodge

19. A - True

20. C - Hagemeister Park

DID YOU KNOW?

1. Russ Letlow was the first player ever drafted by the Green Bay Packers. He was an offensive lineman who played college football at the University of San Francisco. A four-time All-Pro selection, Letlow is one of 10 players named to the National Football League 1930s All-Decade Team who have not been inducted into the Pro Football Hall of Fame.

2. Although Vince Lombardi was known as a disciplinarian, he was also a trendsetter who created an environment that was supportive of both gay and minority players. The architect of the Packers dynasty that won five NFL championships in seven years, Lombardi never posted a losing season as an NFL head coach.

3. Curly Lambeau was a co-founder of the Green Bay Packers franchise and served as head coach and general manager for 30 years. He was the Packers' main offensive weapon during the 1920s and tallied 35 touchdowns as a runner, receiver and passer. Lambeau coached seven future Hall of Fame players and Green Bay renamed its home stadium to Lambeau Field in 1965.

4. The Packers' first sponsor was the Indian Packing Company and the new franchise was called "the Indians" in an early newspaper article. However, the team was known as the "Packers" before its first game. The Acme Packing Company

purchased Indian Packing Co. in 1921 and the squad played its first NFL season with the name "ACME PACKERS" on its jerseys.

5. Bernie Scherer was the first football player from the University of Nebraska to be selected in the NFL draft. He played four seasons of professional football and won an NFL championship in 1936 with the Packers. He served in the U.S. Army during World War II, the Korean War and the Vietnam War.

6. George Svendsen played five seasons for the Packers and is another of the ten players named to the National Football League 1930s All-Decade Team who have not been inducted into the Pro Football Hall of Fame. His brother, Bud, was drafted by Green Bay in 1937; both brothers won a championship title with the Packers – George in 1936 and Bud in 1939. A 6-foot-4 offensive lineman, George also played one season of professional basketball in the National Basketball League.

7. Larry Craig was a two-way player who spent 11 seasons with the Green Bay Packers. He is also one of the first two players to ever be penalized by the league office. NFL commissioner Elmer Layden levied $25 fines on Craig and New York Giant halfback Hank Soar in 1941 for fighting.

8. George Calhoun was a co-founder of the Packers who spent 44 years with the organization. He was an editor at the *Green Bay Press-Gazette* and played a key role in establishing local support for the team. In 1978, he was elected to the Green Bay Packers Hall of Fame.

9. Larry Buhler was the Packers' first-round selection in 1939. He played in just 21 NFL games before retiring two years later. In 1993, a statue of Buhler was erected on the grounds of the Cottonwood County Courthouse in Windom, Minnesota.

10. Historic Lambeau Field has been the home of the Packers for 63 seasons and is the oldest continually operating football stadium in American professional sports. Besides being the fourth-largest stadium on the NFL in normal capacity, it is also the largest venue in Wisconsin. The stadium was renamed in 1965 in memory of Packers co-founder Curly Lambeau.

CHAPTER 2:

JERSEYS & NUMBERS

QUIZ TIME!

1. Which Packers Hall-of-Famer wore No. 83?

    a. Jim Ringo

    b. Walt Kiesling

    c. Len Ford

    d. Willie Davis

2. The original colors of the Green Bay Packers' uniforms were blue and gold.

    a. True

    b. False

3. What does the G on the Packers helmet stand for?

    a. Golden

    b. Greatness

    c. Green Bay

    d. Gridiron

4. I was a player-coach for the Packers who also wore No. 1. Who am I?

    a. Paul Hornung
    b. Whitey Woodin
    c. Curly Lambeau
    d. Herm Schneidman

5. Who was the first Green Bay Packer to have his number retired by the franchise?

    a. Bart Starr
    b. Ray Nitschke
    c. Tony Canadeo
    d. Don Hutson

6. Reggie White was the first NFL player to have his number retired by two teams. Which franchises gave him this honor?

    a. Green Bay & Tampa Bay
    b. Green Bay & New Orleans
    c. Green Bay & Philadelphia
    d. Green Bay & San Francisco

7. Although Paul Hornung's No. 5 was unofficially retired by the Packers in 1967, four other players have worn the number since his retirement.

    a. True
    b. False

8. In 1923, how many thin navy stripes were on each sleeve of the Packers gold jersey?

a. 2

b. 3

c. 6

d. 9

9. What was the year the Packers introduced dark green jerseys for the first time?

a. 1931

b. 1935

c. 1940

d. 1941

10. For two seasons, 1957 and 1958, the Packers wore white helmets with green numbers on both sides.

a. True

b. False

11. Which former Packers kicker wore No. 13 and booted 17 50+ yard field goals during his eight seasons with the franchise?

a. Chris Jacke

b. Al Del Greco

c. Chester Marcol

d. Max Zendejas

12. Who was the most productive Packer to wear No. 84?

a. Fred Nixon

b. Javon Walker

c. Sterling Sharpe

d. Lenny Taylor

13. Which of the following jersey numbers is NOT officially retired by the Packers?

   a. 4
   b. 7
   c. 14
   d. 15

14. The Green Bay Packers gifted halfback Tony Canadeo a car when his jersey was retired in 1952.

   a. True
   b. False

15. Which of the following Packers players did NOT wear No. 99?

   a. John Dorsey
   b. Bruce Gaston
   c. Christian Ringo
   d. Gabe Wilkins

16. What Hall of Fame offensive lineman wore the No. 75 for 15 seasons in Green Bay, but had to wear No. 79 for his final season with Dallas in 1971?

   a. Jerry Kramer
   b. Cal Hubbard
   c. Forrest Gregg
   d. Mike Michalske

17. Two talented wide receivers wore No. 80 for the Packers. Who were they?

a. John Jefferson & Max McGee

b. Boyd Dowler & Billy Howton

c. Don Beebe & Greg Jennings

d. Donald Driver & James Lofton

18. How many Packers players have worn the No. 1 jersey?

a. 1

b. 3

c. 4

d. 6

19. Hall of Fame quarterback Brett Favre wore No. 2 during his rookie season.

a. True

b. False

20. What year did the Packers debut large white numbers on the front of their uniform jerseys?

a. 1928

b. 1930

c. 1934

d. 1937

QUIZ ANSWERS

1. C - Len Ford & Ted Hendricks

2. A - True

3. C – Green Bay

4. C - Curly Lambeau

5. D - Don Hutson

6. C - Green Bay & Philadelphia

7. A - True

8. D - 9

9. B - 1935

10. B - False

11. A - Chris Jacke

12. C - Sterling Sharpe

13. B - 7

14. A - True

15. D - Gabe Wilkins

16. C - Forrest Gregg

17. D - Donald Driver & James Lofton

18. A - 1

19. B - False

20. C – 1934

DID YOU KNOW?

1. John Martinkovic was the only Green Bay Packer listed among the toughest players in the NFL in a 1955 *Life Magazine* feature titled, "Savagery on Sunday." The defensive end was a ferocious hitter in an era known for brutal hits. He wore No. 39 and 83 for the Packers in six seasons with the team and owned a profitable car dealership in Wisconsin.

2. Larry Olsonoski was the first player in the history of the Green Bay Packers to wear No. 74. He was chosen in the sixth round of the 1948 NFL Draft and played parts of two seasons with the franchise. He retired in 1949 after playing in 24 career games with the Packers and New York Bulldogs.

3. Paul Hornung, who wore No. 5 for the Packers, is the only player to win the Heisman Trophy on a losing team. He won the award in 1956 even though Notre Dame had a 2-8 record. He was a two-way standout for the Fighting Irish as a quarterback and safety. Although Hornung's No. 5 has never been officially retired, it has not been issued since 1988.

4. Don Hutson's No. 14 was the first jersey number retired by the Packers in 1951. In 1945, he set an NFL record for most points scored in one quarter. Hutson racked up 29 points on four touchdown catches and five extra points in a windstorm to set a record that had yet to be eclipsed as of 2020.

5. A pair of Pro Football Hall-of-Famers, Cal Hubbard and Clarke Hinkle, both wore No. 27 for the Packers. The first player to wear the number was halfback Myrt Basing in 1927; he scored nine touchdowns in five NFL seasons.

6. Reggie White is the only player to have his number retired posthumously by the Packers. His No. 92 was retired in 2005 in a halftime ceremony at Lambeau Field. White was also the first NFL player to have his number retired by two different organizations, the Packers and the Eagles.

7. The No. 1 jersey is the only Packers jersey that has only been worn by one individual. Packers founder Earl "Curly" Lambeau wore the number for 10 seasons as a player-coach. He scored 35 touchdowns in 77 games as the Packers' main passer and runner and helped the team win the 1929 NFL title in his final year as a player.

8. Offensive lineman Walt Jean became the first Packer to wear No. 8 in 1925. He might also have been the only black player to ever play for Curly Lambeau. The Oldest Living Pro Football Players website reports that Jean may have been an African-American posing as a white man when he played two years for the Packers. Jean also played with Jim Thorpe on a team called the Portsmouth Shoe-Steels.

9. Three Pro Football Hall-of-Famers — Herb Adderley, Arnie Herber and Johnny "Blood" McNally — have worn No. 26 for the Packers. Claude Perry was the first Packer ever to wear the number.

10. No. 57 Ken Bowman was the Packers center in 1967 when

Bart Starr scored on a quarterback sneak in the Ice Bowl to help Green Bay win their third straight NFL championship. He was arrested during the 1974 players strike and sat out the 1974 season after being put on injured reserve with a non-existent back injury.

CHAPTER 3:

PACKERS QUARTERBACKS

QUIZ TIME!

1. In what round did the Packers select QB Bart Starr in the 1956 NFL Draft?

   a. 10th
   b. 12th
   c. 17th
   d. 19th

2. Although Green Bay quarterback Arnie Herber was the first great long thrower in the NFL, he never led the league in passing yards.

   a. True
   b. False

3. Aaron Rodgers broke the record for the highest single-season passer rating with a 122.5. What year did he set the record?

   a. 2005
   b. 2007

c. 2011

d. 2014

4. Brett Favre completed his first pass as a Packer to a non-receiver. Who was that player?

   a. James Campen

   b. Brett Favre

   c. Tootie Robbins

   d. Ken Ruettgers

5. Who was the first quarterback in the history of the Green Bay Packers?

   a. Norm Barry

   b. Red Dunn

   c. Adolph Kliebhan

   d. Charlie Mathys

6. Packers quarterback Irv Comp was the NFL passing yards leader in 1944.

   a. True

   b. False

7. Which of the following Packers had both his high school and college jerseys retired?

   a. Brett Favre

   b. Bart Starr

   c. Lynn Dickey

   d. Aaron Rodgers

8. Who was the first Packers quarterback to have more than 100 pass completions in a single season?

a. Cecil Isbell

b. Bart Starr

c. Arnie Herber

d. Tony Canadeo

9. During my seven years with the Packers, I ranked first in the NFL in rushing yards by a quarterback. Who am I?

a. Tobin Rote

b. Bullet Baker

c. Brett Favre

d. Don Majkowski

10. Don Majkowski earned a new contract by throwing 27 touchdown passes and leading the NFL with 4,318 passing yards in 1989.

a. True

b. False

11. Which of the following players shared starting quarterback duties with Lynn Dickey, Jim Zorn and Don Majkowski?

a. Matt Flynn

b. Alan Risher

c. Mike Tomczak

d. Randy Wright

12. Which team drafted Brett Favre in the second round of the 1991 NFL Draft?

a. Atlanta Falcons

b. Detroit Lions

c. Buffalo Bills

d. Green Bay Packers

13. Which of the following Green Bay quarterbacks passed for 4,458 yards in a single season?

   a. Bart Starr

   b. Brett Favre

   c. Lynn Dickey

   d. Aaron Rodgers

14. The Packers drafted UCLA standout Brett Hundley in the fifth round of the 2015 NFL Draft.

   a. True

   b. False

15. Who was the first NFL quarterback to complete 6,000 passes, complete 500 touchdown passes and throw for 70,000 yards?

   a. Bart Starr

   b. Brett Favre

   c. Arnie Herber

   d. Aaron Rodgers

16. In 2013, I became the first African-American to start a game as quarterback for the Green Bay Packers. Who am I?

   a. Reggie Collier

   b. Brett Hundley

   c. Seneca Wallace

   d. Charlie Brackins

17. Which quarterback guided the Packers to victories in Super Bowl I and II?

    a. John Hadl
    b. Bart Starr
    c. Babe Parilli
    d. John Roach

18. Which former Green Bay quarterback retired after being selected in the third round of the 2019 Alliance of American Football Quarterback Draft?

    a. Scott Tolzien
    b. Blair Kiel
    c. Matt Flynn
    d. Mike Tomczak

19. Bart Starr holds the Packers team record for most passing yards in a season.

    a. True
    b. False

20. Who is the only Packer to win the Associated Press NFL Most Valuable Player Award three consecutive years?

    c. Bart Starr
    d. Don Hutson
    e. Brett Favre
    f. Aaron Rodgers

QUIZ ANSWERS

1. C - 17th

2. B - False

3. C - 2011

4. B - Brett Favre

5. C - Adolph Kliebhan

6. A - True

7. C - Lynn Dickey

8. A - Cecil Isbell

9. A - Tobin Rote

10. A - True

11. D - Randy Wright

12. A - Atlanta Falcons

13. C - Lynn Dickey

14. A - True

15. B - Brett Favre

16. C - Seneca Wallace

17. B - Bart Starr

18. A - Scott Tolzien

19. B - False

20. C - Brett Favre

DID YOU KNOW?

1. Willie Wood was a junior college All-American who transferred to the University of Southern California to become the first African-American quarterback to play in what is now the Pac-12 Conference. He signed with the Packers as an undrafted free agent and switched to safety during his rookie year. Wood was a five-time first-team All-Pro safety and is a member of the Pro Football Hall of Fame.

2. During a hazing incident at the University of Alabama, Bart Starr suffered a significant back injury in 1954 and missed most of his junior season. However, he falsely claimed that he hurt his back while punting a football. The injury resulted in Starr not being able to serve in the Vietnam War.

3. Brett Favre was involved in a horrible car accident in 1990 that caused doctors to remove 30 inches of his small intestine. Favre's car flipped three times when he lost control going around a bend in Mississippi. However, Favre made a full recovery and led Southern Mississippi to a comeback win over Alabama six weeks after his near-fatal car crash.

4. Aaron Rodgers was a freshman at Butte Community College when he was accidentally discovered by the California Golden Bears. While scouting Butte tight end

Garrett Cross, Bears head coach Jeff Tedford was impressed with Rodgers. The future Packers quarterback transferred to the University of California the following season.

5. Ingle Martin was the Packers third-string quarterback in 2006 behind starter Brett Favre and backup Aaron Rodgers. Although he was in the league for three seasons, he only made one appearance in an NFL game for just two offensive plays.

6. Lamar McHan was the Packers starting quarterback in 1959 after being traded by the Chicago Cardinals for insubordination. He started the first six games before shoulder and leg injuries resulted in Bart Starr taking the helms of the offense. He was a single-wing tailback at the University of Arkansas and finished ninth in the 1953 Heisman Trophy race.

7. Jim McMahon won his second Super Bowl championship with the Green Bay Packers as the backup for starting quarterback Brett Favre. He retired following Super Bowl XXXI, which was played in the same venue – the New Orleans Superdome – where he celebrated his first NFL title with the Bears in Super Bowl XX.

8. Perry Moss started only one game for the Packers during his lone season in the NFL. He compiled an 0-9-1 record at Marshall University in 1968 but resigned due to alleged recruiting violations. However, dozens of team members petitioned to have Moss reinstated as their coach the following season. Fortunately for Moss, the petition was

denied, and the university hired an interim coach. The following season, the Marshall football team perished in a plane crash.

9. Craig Nall was a Packers 2002 fifth-round draft choice who was the top passer in NFL Europe in 2003 with the Scottish Claymores. The following season, he threw for 314 yards and 4 touchdowns as the second-string quarterback behind Brett Favre.

10. Rick Norton played only one game for the Packers but he is in the record books for throwing the last professional touchdown pass at Wrigley Field. In a 1970 matchup against the Chicago Bears, he tossed a 29-yard strike to John Hilton late in the fourth quarter. It was the last time that a professional football game was played at the historic field in Chicago.

CHAPTER 4:

THE PASS CATCHERS

QUIZ TIME!

1. I scored 825 points in my career and revolutionized the position of wide receiver. What was my name?

   a. Joel Mason

   b. Ray Riddick

   c. Don Hutson

   d. Harry Jacunski

2. Jordy Nelson set a franchise record in 2014 for most receiving yards in a season.

   a. True

   b. False

3. Which of the following players was voted the winner of season 14 of Dancing with the Stars?

   a. James Jones

   b. Javon Walker

   c. Donald Driver

   d. Greg Jennings

4. In 1992, Sterling Sharpe became only the eighth wide receiver in NFL history to achieve this rare feat. What did he accomplish?

    a. Rookie of the Year Award
    b. Receiving Triple Crown
    c. Unanimous All-Pro Selection
    d. Most Valuable Player Award

5. I caught a touchdown pass and set the Packers' rookie record with 117 receiving yards in a 2015 playoff game. Who am I?

    a. Randall Cobb
    b. Greg Jennings
    c. Jarrett Boykin
    d. Davante Adams

6. Randall Cobb was the first person born in the 1990s to play in the NFL.

    a. True
    b. False

7. Which Packers receiver caught a pass on his back and got up to score a touchdown in a catch that was labeled the greatest play in the history of Monday Night Football?

    a. James Lofton
    b. Antonio Freeman
    c. Donald Driver
    d. Robert Brooks

8. Which one of the following Packers was also an NCAA long jump champion at Stanford University?

a. Carroll Dale

b. Steve Odom

c. James Lofton

d. John Jefferson

9. Don Hutson's first reception in the NFL was a touchdown pass from Arnie Herber on the first play from scrimmage. How long was his touchdown catch?

a. 83 yards

b. 70 yards

c. 80 yards

d. 73 yards

10. Besides his time with the Packers, Jordy Nelson also played one season for the Los Angeles Chargers.

a. True

b. False

11. Which Packer caught Brett Favre's first completion to a wide receiver?

a. Perry Kemp

b. Mark Clayton

c. Sterling Sharpe

d. Sanjay Beach

12. How many touchdowns did Don Hutson score in his rookie year?

a. 5

b. 0

c. 6

d. 2

13. Which player ignored Green Bay coach Forrest Gregg's instructions to fair-catch a punt and scored an 83-yard touchdown to win the game?

    a. Terry Glenn
    b. Boyd Dowler
    c. Walter Stanley
    d. Mark Ingram, Sr.

14. Hall of Fame receiver Don Hutson credited playing with snakes as a Boy Scout for his quickness and agility.

    a. True
    b. False

15. Which Packers receiver caught 102 passes in 1995?

    a. Randall Cobb
    b. Robert Brooks
    c. John Jefferson
    d. Antonio Freeman

16. I wore a green hooded sweatshirt underneath my jersey in a chilly game in Minnesota which resulted in the NFL adding a new rule banning hoodies under jerseys. Who am I?

    a. James Jones
    b. James Lofton
    c. Greg Jennings
    d. Donald Driver

17. What was the most touchdown passes that Sterling Sharpe caught in a single season?

a. 13

b. 18

c. 15

d. 19

18. Don Hutson was an eight-time First-team All-Pro who led the NFL in catches eight different seasons. How many times did he lead the league in receiving touchdowns?

a. 3

b. 5

c. 9

d. 6

19. Davante Adams was the first wide receiver taken in the 2014 NFL Draft.

a. True

b. False

20. Who was the first rookie in Packers history to return both a kick and a punt for a touchdown in the same season?

c. Jordy Nelson

d. James Jones

e. Randall Cobb

f. Greg Jennings

QUIZ ANSWERS

1. C - Don Hutson

2. A - True

3. C - Donald Driver

4. B – Receiving Triple Crown

5. D - Davante Adams

6. A - True

7. B - Antonio Freeman

8. C - James Lofton

9. A - 83 yards

10. B - False

11. D - Sanjay Beach

12. C - 6

13. C - Walter Stanley

14. A - True

15. B - Robert Brooks

16. A - James Jones

17. B - 18

18. C - 9

19. B - False

20. C - Randall Cobb

DID YOU KNOW?

1. Don Hutson's first catch as an NFL receiver was an 83-yard touchdown pass from Arnie Herber against the Chicago Bears. He led the league in touchdowns in nine seasons and in receiving yards seven times. Hutson held 14 of the league's 15 pass-catching records when he retired in 1945.

2. Devante Adams suffered a pair of brutal concussions during the 2018 season. He was taken to the hospital after a helmet-to-helmet collision with Bears linebacker Danny Trevathan in a Week 4 contest. Adams suffered another helmet-to-helmet hit from Panthers linebacker Thomas Davis in Week 15 that led him to miss the final two games of the regular season.

3. Devin Funchess started his career at the University of Michigan as a tight end who wore No. 87, but he switched to No. 1 during his junior campaign when he moved to wide receiver. Funchess was the first Wolverine receiver to wear the number since 2004.

4. Packers wide receiver Equanimeous St. Brown holds both American and German citizenship. His father, John Brown, won the Mr. Universe title in 1981 and 1982 and was also a three-time Mr. World champion. He was one of the biggest stars in bodybuilding during his career.

5. Jared Abbrederis was drafted in the fifth round in 2014 and was the first player from the University of Wisconsin

to be selected by the Packers in 13 years. However, the wide receiver missed his entire rookie season after tearing his ACL during training camp.

6. Mark Chmura did not join his Packers teammates on a trip to the White House after the team won Super Bowl XXXI because he was participating in the annual Mike Utley golf tournament. Despite claims that Chmura did not attend the 1997 event with U.S. President Bill Clinton because of his Republican background, the former tight end had competed in the charity golf tournament since 1992.

7. John Jefferson was the first player in league history to gain 1,000 receiving yards in each of his first three NFL seasons. In 1979, the talented wide receiver was featured on the cover of *Sports Illustrated* as "The Touchdown Man."

8. Packers wide receiver Jake Kumerow possesses an extraordinary football pedigree. His father Eric is a former Miami Dolphins linebacker and his uncle is former Dolphins defensive end John Bosa. Thus, he is the cousin of Los Angeles Chargers defensive end Joey Bosa and San Francisco 49ers defensive end Nick Bosa.

9. James Lofton is a Pro Football Hall-of-Famer who is one of the most decorated receivers of all time. He was the first NFL player to record 14,000 yards receiving and was the second player to score a touchdown in the 1970's, 1980's and 1990's. Lofton was selected to play in seven Pro Bowls during his nine seasons with the Packers.

10. Red Mack spent only one season in Green Bay but

contributed two special team tackles in Super Bowl I. Although he played only six years in the NFL, he endured two knee replacements and two hip replacements and also had one of his shoulders replaced.

CHAPTER 5:

RUNNING WILD

QUIZ TIME!

1. Who was the first running back in franchise history to rush for over 1,000 yards in a season?

   a. Jim Taylor
   b. Kenneth Davis
   c. Tony Canadeo
   d. Eddie Lee Ivery

2. From 2000 to 2004, Ahman Green rushed for more yards than any other NFL running back.

   a. True
   b. False

3. Which rookie running back led the Packers in rushing in 1986?

   a. Gerry Ellis
   b. Keith Woodside
   c. Eddie Lee Ivery
   d. Kenneth Davis

4. I played wide receiver at Stanford University, but was switched to running back during my second season with the Packers? Who am I?

   a. Brent Fullwood
   b. Ty Montgomery
   c. Brandon Jackson
   d. Eric Torkelson

5. Who was the first NFL player to rush for 1,000 or more yards in each of his first three seasons?

   a. John Brockington
   b. Ahman Green
   c. Eddie Lacy
   d. Eddie Lee Ivery

6. Green Bay Packers Hall-of-Famer Jim Taylor had his No. 31 jersey retired by the Saints.

   a. True
   b. False

7. Which Packers running back tore his Achilles tendon while volunteering at a football camp for underserved youth and never played in the NFL again?

   a. Ted Fritsch
   b. Gerry Ellis
   c. MacArthur Lane
   d. Terdell Middleton

8. Despite being the 19th running back selected in the 2017 NFL Draft, I led the league in rushing touchdowns two years later. Who am I?

a. Eddie Lacy

b. Aaron Jones

c. Jamaal Williams

d. Ty Montgomery

9. What Packers running back rushed for 8,207 career yards and a franchise-record 81 rushing touchdowns?

a. Ahman Green

b. Clarke Hinkle

c. Jim Taylor

d. Paul Hornung

10. Apart from Paul Hornung, every Packer on the team roster played in Super Bowl I.

a. True

b. False

11. Which one of the following players was on the cover of Madden NFL 2000, and is considered one of the first victims of the "Madden Curse."

a. Ahman Green

b. Travis Jervey

c. Dorsey Levens

d. Edgar Bennett

12. I rushed for 201 rushing yards in a divisional playoff game win against the Seattle Seahawks to set a franchise record. Who am I?

a. Ryan Grant

b. Gerry Ellis

c. Eddie Lacy

d. Terdell Middleton

13. Which undrafted free agent set a Packers rookie record by rushing for 171 yards against the Detroit Lions?

a. Samkon Gado

b. Aaron Jones

c. Ahman Green

d. Jim Taylor

14. Who had a 98-yard run that is the longest rushing play in the history of the Packers?

a. Joe Laws

b. Ryan Grant

c. Ahman Green

d. Charley Brock

15. Vince Workman set the Green Bay Packers team record for most receptions by a running back in a single game. How many catches did he have?

a. 10

b. 12

c. 15

d. 16

16. What former Packer outran Herschel Walker in the 1996 NFL's Fastest Man competition?

a. Ahman Green

b. Travis Jervey

c. James Starks

d. Reggie Cobb

17. Which of the following players is the all-time leading rusher in Packers history?

    a. Jim Taylor
    b. Tony Canadeo
    c. Ahman Green
    d. John Brockington

18. Which team selected Paul Hornung in the 1967 NFL expansion draft?

    a. Chicago Bears
    b. Detroit Lions
    c. Kansas City Chiefs
    d. New Orleans Saints

19. Kenneth Davis missed his entire senior season at TCU when he was suspended after receiving cash payments from boosters.

    a. True
    b. False

20. Which Packers running back said, "Football is a contact sport. You've got to make them respect you. You've got to punish tacklers. You've got to deal out more misery than the tacklers deal out to you"?

    c. Jim Taylor
    d. Paul Hornung
    e. Dorsey Levens
    f. Edgar Bennett

QUIZ ANSWERS

1. C - Tony Canadeo

2. A - True

3. D - Kenneth Davis

4. B - Ty Montgomery

5. A - John Brockington

6. A - True

7. B - Gerry Ellis

8. B - Aaron Jones

9. C - Jim Taylor

10. A - True

11. C - Dorsey Levens

12. A - Ryan Grant

13. A - Samkon Gado

14. C – Ahman Green

15. B - 12

16. B - Travis Jervey

17. C - Ahman Green

18. D - New Orleans Saints

19. B - False

20. A - Jim Taylor

DID YOU KNOW?

1. Dave Kopay was a special teams standout who played his final season in the NFL with the Packers. He was the first former NFL player to come out as being gay. His best season came during his rookie year when he rushed for 271 yards and caught 20 passes for the 49ers.

2. Elijah Pitts spurned the AFL's Boston Patriots in 1961 and signed with the Packers for less money. Although he spent most of his career as a backup to running back Paul Hornung, he scored two touchdowns in Super Bowl I, when the "Golden Boy" was sidelined with a pinched nerve.

3. Despite missing parts of the 2014 season and the entire 2015 season at Brigham Young, Jamaal Williams rushed for a school-record 3,901 yards with 35 touchdowns. He also shattered the school record for most rushing yards in a single game in 2016 with 286 yards and 5 touchdowns in a win over Toledo.

4. Vince Workman once held the record for most catches by a running back in a single game for two different NFL franchises. He set the mark for the Packers in 1992 with 12 receptions against the Minnesota Vikings. Three years later, he set the same record for the Carolina Panthers and it stood until Christian McCaffrey caught 15 passes in a 2019 game.

5. DeShawn Wynn was a 2002 *Parade* magazine high school

All-American who was tabbed as one of the top running backs in the country. He rushed for more than 2,000 yards on three different occasions and scored 30 touchdowns during his senior year. He was also a member of the Florida Gators' BCS National Championship team in the 2006 season.

6. Donny Anderson was a halfback and punter for the Packers who is credited with introducing the concept of hang time in punting to the NFL. The left-footed punter focused on punting the ball higher, which allowed his teammates more time to get down the field. In 1967, he punted 63 times and opposing teams only managed 13 punt returns for 22 yards.

7. Khalil Bell was an undrafted free agent who spent his final season of pro football with the Packers. He set a league record in 2009 when he raced 72 yards on his first NFL carry against the Philadelphia Eagles. His record stood for seven years until the Oakland Raiders Jalen Richards ripped off a 75-yard touchdown run on his first NFL carry.

8. Edgar Bennett was a productive NFL running back who finished his career with nearly 4,000 rushing yards and 284 receptions. He also served as offensive coordinator for the Packers for three seasons to become one of the few African-Americans to hold that position.

9. Michael Blair was an undrafted free agent who played in 13 NFL games with the Packers and Cincinnati Bengals. He has appeared in two Hollywood films – "We Are Marshall,'

starring Matthew McConaughey and "The Game Plan," starring Dwayne "Rock" Johnson – as a football player.

10. Najeh Davenport was an injury-prone running back who was oozing with athletic talent. He ran for 178 yards in his first NFL start, which was the third-highest debut for a running back at the time in the previous 20 years. The University of Miami product also scored two touchdowns in his only start in 2005, but he broke his ankle in that game and was placed on injured reserve.

CHAPTER 6:

IN THE TRENCHES

QUIZ TIME!

1. What Green Bay offensive lineman wrote a book called *Instant Replay*?

    a. Ken Gray

    b. Jerry Kramer

    c. Len St. Jean

    d. Ken Bowman

2. The Packers' 2016 second-round draft pick, Jason Spriggs, was 6-foot-6 and weighed 249 pounds coming out of high school.

    a. True

    b. False

3. What was the name of the Packers offensive lineman who started 162 consecutive games and was nicknamed the "Rock" because he rarely missed a game?

    a. Bill Bain

    b. Keith Wortman

c. Larry McCarren

d. Derrel Gofourth

4. Which of these former Packers went to medical school part-time during his playing days and became an orthopedic surgeon when his football career ended?

a. Kevin Hunt

b. Bill Hayhoe

c. Mark Koncar

d. Malcolm Snider

5. What overall draft pick did the Packers use to select Michigan State offensive tackle Tony Mandarich in the 1989 NFL Draft?

a. 2nd

b. 4th

c. 5th

d. 7th

6. David Bakhtiari was the only NFL rookie to start every game at left tackle during the 2013 season.

a. True

b. False

7. Which of the following offensive linemen was credited with not allowing a single sack on 571 pass-blocking snaps in his rookie season?

a. Corey Linsley

b. Elgton Jenkins

c. J.C. Tretter

d. Derek Sherrod

8. What is the name of the Packers player who had a 16-hour drinking contest against professional wrestler Lex Luger?

   a. Greg Koch
   b. Karl Swanke
   c. Leotis Harris
   d. Tim Huffman

9. In 2006, the Packers drafted Boise State guard Daryn Colledge in the second round with the 47th pick. He was the highest-ever selection from what state?

   a. Idaho
   b. Maine
   c. Wyoming
   d. Alaska

10. The Green Bay Packers drafted Holy Cross center Jon Morris in 1964, but he spurned the franchise and signed with the Dallas Cowboys.

    a. True
    b. False

11. Which one of the following Packers finished his career with the Chicago Fire of the World Football League?

    a. Bill Lueck
    b. Dick Himes
    c. Dave Bradley
    d. Melvin Jackson

12. Packers Hall-of-Famer Jerry Kramer auctioned off his Super Bowl I ring in 2016 to send his grandchildren to college. How much was the ring sold for?

a. $100,000

b. $125,000

c. $200,000

d. $250,000

13. Which of the following Green Bay offensive linemen worked at Argonne National Laboratories and researched nuclear magnetic resonance?

a. Andy Cvercko

b. Ed Blaine

c. John Gilliam

d. Dan Grimm

14. Green Bay offensive tackle Steve Wright was the model for the Walter Payton NFL Man of the Year Award.

a. True

b. False

15. In 2016, what former Packer announced that he had enlisted in the Idaho Army National Guard?

a. Rich Moran

b. Mark Cannon

c. Daryn Colledge

d. Ron Hallstrom

16. Which of the following Packers was the first rookie to ever start a Super Bowl at left tackle when Green Bay played the Denver Broncos in Super Bowl XXXII?

a. Aaron Taylor

b. Ken Ruettgers

c. Adam Timmerman

d. Ross Verba

17. Which Green Bay offensive tackle was severely injured by a blindside hit from Tampa Bay Buccaneers defensive tackle Warren Sapp, which led to updated guidelines for "unnecessary roughness" penalties?

a. Chad Clifton

b. Marco Rivera

c. Mark Tauscher

d. Mike Flanagan

18. John Michels was the Packers' first-round selection in the 1996 NFL Draft. What was his profession after he retired from pro football?

a. Stockbroker

b. Insurance agent

c. High school principal

d. Pain management physician

19. Green Bay Hall-of-Famer Jerry Kramer was also a placekicker known as "the best knuckleball kicker in the NFL."

a. True

b. False

20. Which offensive tackle suffered a torn ACL injury at the Packers' Family Night intrasquad scrimmage during the 2013 training camp?

a. J.C. Tretter

b. Bryan Bulaga
c. David Bakhtiari
d. Marshall Newhouse

QUIZ ANSWERS

1. B - Jerry Kramer
2. A - True
3. C - Larry McCarren
4. D - Malcolm Snider
5. A - 2nd
6. A - True
7. B - Elgton Jenkins
8. A - Greg Koch
9. D - Alaska
10. B - False
11. C - Dave Bradley
12. B - $125,000
13. A - Andy Cvercko
14. A - True
15. C - Daryn Colledge
16. D - Ross Verba
17. A - Chad Clifton
18. D - Pain management physician
19. A - True
20. B - Bryan Bulaga

DID YOU KNOW?

1. Legendary Green Bay offensive lineman Jerry Kramer was also occasionally a placekicker for the Packers. The Pro Football Hall-of-Famer is an accomplished author who has written several Packers-related books. His first book, *Instant Replay*, was named the 20th greatest sports book of all time by *Sports Illustrated* in 2002.

2. Forrest Gregg played in an amazing 188 consecutive games for the Packers from 1956 to 1970. He was a nine-time Pro Bowl selection who spent 11 seasons as an NFL head coach with the Cleveland Browns, Cincinnati Bengals and the Packers.

3. Keith Uecker was the Packers' recipient of the Ed Block Courage Award in 1987. That same year, he became the only member of the Packers to cross the picket line and play with the replacement players during the players' strike. Two years later, he was suspended by the NFL for steroid use.

4. Evan Smith was the Packers offensive lineman who was stomped on by Lions defensive tackle Ndamukong Suh during a Thanksgiving Day contest in 2011. His teammate, Matt Brock, has alleged that Smith and another offensive lineman provoked Suh by constantly untying his shoes.

5. Jug Earp's father was the cousin of legendary lawman and gambler, Wyatt Earp. Like his famous cousin, Jug enjoyed

success in his profession as a member of the Packers dynasty that won three consecutive NFL championships from 1929 to 1931.

6. Tunch Ilkin, the first native of Turkey to play in the NFL, spent only one season with the Packers. Besides several television gigs in the Pittsburgh area, he directs a multi-site church, Men's Ministries for The Bible Chapel.

7. Syd Kitson was a backup guard for the Packers who suffered two severe injuries early in his career. The former third-round pick missed five games with a neck injury in 1981 and was back on the injured reserve the following year after getting his shoulder cracked during a preseason game.

8. Tony Mandarich was the second overall pick in the 1989 NFL Draft and is the only one of the top five picks in his draft class who is not in the Pro Football Hall of Fame. He was drafted behind Troy Aikman, but ahead of Barry Sanders, Derrick Thomas and Deion Sanders.

9. Jon Runyan Jr., the Packers' 2020 sixth-round draft pick, is the son of former NFL offensive tackle Jon Runyan. His father was considered one of the dirtiest players in the league and became the fourth NFL player to be elected to Congress in 2010.

10. Derek Sherrod was the Packers' first-round pick in 2011 and was expected to anchor the offensive line for many years. However, he broke his right leg during his rookie season and was not on the active roster again until late in

2013. In 2010, he graduated from Mississippi State with a 3.54 grade-point average and was a finalist for the William V. Campbell Trophy, known as the Academic Heisman.

CHAPTER 7:

THE BACK SEVEN

QUIZ TIME!

1. How many sacks did Packers outside linebacker Clay Matthews have during his rookie year?

   a. 10
   b. 11
   c. 12
   d. 13

2. The Packers' 2019 first-round draft pick Rashan Gary was ranked as college football's No. 1 recruit coming out of high school

   a. True
   b. False

3. Which Packers linebacker was offered a contract with a $3,000 signing bonus to play baseball for the St. Louis Browns?

   a. Brian Noble
   b. Ray Nitschke

c. George Cumby

d. John Anderson

4. Green Bay selected a safety with the 21st pick of the 2014 NFL Draft and issued him No. 21, which was previously worn by Charles Woodson. Who was this defensive back?

a. Micah Hyde

b. Casey Heyward

c. Damarious Randall

d. Ha Ha Clinton-Dix

5. Who was the former Packers safety who was given a 20-year prison sentence in 2016 after pleading guilty to multiple rape and drug-related charges?

a. Ahmad Carroll

b. Will Blackmon

c. Darren Sharper

d. Antuan Edwards

6. Clay Matthews, whose father played 19 seasons in the NFL, is the nephew of Pro Football Hall of Fame offensive lineman Bruce Matthews.

a. True

b. False

7. The Packers traded cornerback Craig Newsome two years after he intercepted a pass in Super Bowl XXXI. What was the team that traded for him?

a. San Francisco 49ers

b. Seattle Seahawks

c. Tampa Bay Buccaneers

d. Washington Redskins

8. Hall of Fame cornerback Herb Adderley began his NFL career as an offensive player. What position did he play before being switched to defense?

a. Guard

b. Center

c. Halfback

d. Tight End

9. What is the name of the podcast hosted by former Packers linebacker A.J. Hawk?

a. Hawk Talk

b. The HawkCast

c. Hawk Sports Chat

d. Hawk SportsCast

10. Hall of Fame linebacker Dave Robinson earned the name "Lefty" in high school because he was a left-footed kicker.

a. True

b. False

11. Why did opposing quarterbacks target Packers cornerback Ahmad Carroll, who was chosen in the first round of the 2004 NFL Draft?

a. Lack of speed

b. Mental errors

c. Bad fundamentals

d. Contact penalties

12. Which of the following Packers linebackers retired as the franchise all-time leader in tackles and was tied for the Packers' career mark for most interceptions by a linebacker?

    a. Ray Nitschke
    b. Tom Macleod
    c. John Anderson
    d. Mike Douglass

13. Terrell Suggs and Calvin Pace were the first two linebackers selected in the 2003 NFL Draft. Who was the third linebacker taken in the draft that year by the Packers with the 29th pick?

    a. A.J. Hawk
    b. Nick Barnett
    c. Brady Poppinga
    d. Hunter Hillenmeyer

14. The Green Bay Packers selected three consecutive defensive backs the 1999 NFL Draft.

    a. True
    b. False

15. What was the prize that Ray Nitschke received for being the MVP of the 1962 NFL Championship Game?

    a. $10,000
    b. Rolex watch
    c. John Deere tractor
    d. 1963 Chevrolet Corvette

16. Who was the first Packers defensive back to grab more than 50 career interceptions?

    a. LeRoy Butler
    b. Bobby Dillon
    c. Terrell Buckley
    d. Hank Gremminger

17. What injury did Hall of Fame linebacker John Anderson suffer in both 1978 and 1979?

    a. Broken arm
    b. Groin pull
    c. High ankle sprain
    d. Pulled hamstring

18. What linebacker did Green Bay select in the 1968 NFL Draft after trading Hall of Fame fullback Jim Taylor to the New Orleans Saints for the fifth overall draft pick?

    a. Jim Flanigan
    b. Fred Carr
    c. Dave Robinson
    d. Tommy Crutcher

19. Herb Adderley is the only player to appear in five of the first six NFL championship games and Super Bowls.

    a. True
    b. False

20. Which the following Packers played both offense and defense in college, and is the only primarily defensive player to win the Heisman Trophy?

a. Jim Taylor
b. Herb Adderley
c. Charles Woodson
d. John Brockington

QUIZ ANSWERS

1. A - 10

2. A - True

3. B - Ray Nitschke

4. D - Ha Ha Clinton-Dix

5. C - Darren Sharper

6. A - True

7. A - San Francisco 49ers

8. C - Halfback

9. B - The HawkCast

10. A - True

11. D - Contact penalties

12. C - John Anderson

13. B - Nick Barnett

14. A - True

15. D - 1963 Chevrolet Corvette

16. B – Bobby Dan Dillon

17. A - Broken arm

18. B - Fred Carr

19. B - False

20. C - Charles Woodson

DID YOU KNOW?

1. Ray Nitschke stayed busy after his football career ended and appeared in two Hollywood movies as a football player. He also had a successful car dealership and starred in his own television commercials with his pet dog.

2. Torrance Marshall was an exceptional athletic talent who helped the Oklahoma Sooners win the national championship. He was named the MVP of the 2001 Orange Bowl and played four seasons with the Packers. His uncle, Henry Clayton, also played in the NFL.

3. Derrick Martin was a defensive back who was better known for his exceptional play on special teams. He played for the Packers in 2009 and 2010. His home was robbed by a pair of masked men in 2013 while Martin was playing for the Patriots in the AFC Championship Game against the Baltimore Ravens.

4. Clay Matthews was an unheralded, walk-on student-athlete at USC who turned down several playing opportunities during garbage time of games to preserve his remaining years of NCAA eligibility. He was a special team ace who was granted a full athletic scholarship status at the beginning of the 2006 season.

5. Mike McKenzie was a talented cornerback whose career was derailed by a pair of significant knee injuries. He tore his ACL in 2007 but rebounded to start six games the

following season before fracturing his right kneecap. After he retired, he founded a winery that makes wine from orange Moscato grapes.

6. Brian Noble is an avid hunter and fisherman who produced and starred in his own outdoor television show after his pro football career was over called "Hitting the Outdoors." The show was broadcasted mainly throughout the Midwest.

7. Julius Peppers was a member of both the football team and the men's basketball team for several seasons at the University of North Carolina. He tallied 10 rebounds and scored 21 points against the Penn State Nittany Lions in a second-round NCAA Tournament game in 2001.

8. Dave Robinson ended up playing in Green Bay, but he was also drafted by the AFL's San Diego Chargers. However, the Chargers were low on funds and had decided to trade his rights to the Buffalo Bills. Although his future wife had been to Buffalo, she had never been to Wisconsin. Robinson's wife did not join him in Green Bay until his second year in the NFL.

9. Allen Rossum is considered one of the top return specialists in the history of the NFL. He played 12 years in the league with the Packers and four other teams. He was a skilled punt and kickoff return man who is the only player in NFL history to have a kickoff return for a touchdown with five different teams.

10. Chris Akins was a promising safety who developed into a

special team ace with the Packers and several other NFL teams. He had two stints with Green Bay but was released during the 2001 season due to erratic play and misconduct off the field.

CHAPTER 8:

ODDS & ENDS & AWARDS

QUIZ TIME!

1. Which Packer invented the "Lambeau Leap"?

   a. Brett Favre

   b. LeRoy Butler

   c. Robert Brooks

   d. Donald Driver

2. Most of the Packer cheerleaders in 1931 were high school students.

   a. True

   b. False

3. Who was the only Packer to score 5 touchdowns in one game during the 20th century?

   a. Jim Taylor

   b. Paul Hornung

   c. Kenneth Davis

   d. Tony Canadeo

4. How much was Reggie White's contract worth when the Packers signed him as a free agent in 1993?

   a. $14 million
   b. $16 million
   c. $17 million
   d. $19 million

5. In 1929, the Green Bay Packers went undefeated with a 12-0-1 record to capture their first NFL championship. How many points did their incredible defense allow that season?

   a. 13
   b. 37
   c. 30
   d. 22

6. Green Bay is one of only five NFL teams that does not have an official mascot.

   a. True
   b. False

7. Which pair of Packers teammates once bought a pet lion at a store in Dallas?

   a. Jim Taylor & Paul Hornung
   b. Travis Jervey & LeShon Johnson
   c. Jerry Kramer & Forrest Greg
   d. Ted Hendricks & Larry McCarren

8. Who succeeded the legendary Vince Lombardi as head coach of the Packers?

   a. Bart Starr

b. Phil Bengtson

c. Dan Devine

d. Lindy Infante

9. How far was the longest punt by a Packer in franchise history?

    a. 85 yards

    b. 88 yards

    c. 90 yards

    d. 95 yards

10. Greg Jennings caught Brett Favre's 420th touchdown pass, which tied Dan Marino's all-time mark, and Aaron Rodgers' first touchdown toss.

    a. True

    b. False

11. Who was the Packers coach who led the team to five consecutive winning seasons during his tenure from 2000-2005?

    a. Mike McCarthy

    b. Mike Sherman

    c. Lindy Infante

    d. Mike Holmgren

12. What do fans of the Green Bay Packers call themselves?

    a. Cheeseheads

    b. Wolfpack

    c. Cheese Curs

    d. Lambeau Loonies

13. Which of the following players has NOT played for the Packers?

    a. Ken Stills
    b. Mike Prior
    c. Cliff Harris
    d. Johnnie Gray

14. The Green Bay Packers are the only team in NFL history to win four consecutive league championships.

    a. True
    b. False

15. Green Bay was a dominant team in the NFL in the late 1920s and early 1930s and won three consecutive NFL championships. How many consecutive home games did the Packers go without a loss?

    a. 29
    b. 32
    c. 22
    d. 19

16. Which of the following Green Bay head coaches was at the helm of the Packers for the longest time?

    a. Dan Devine
    b. Mike McCarthy
    c. Vince Lombardi
    d. Earl "Curly" Lambeau

17. The Packers won two games by the score of 49-0 in 1962. Which teams did they defeat?

a. Kansas City Chiefs & New York Giants

b. Detroit Lions & Baltimore Colts

c. Chicago Bears and Philadelphia Eagles

d. Washington Redskins & Dallas Texans

18. What is the name of the Green Bay touchdown celebration?

a. Pack Attack

b. Cheezy Hop

c. Green Bay Shuffle

d. Lambeau Leap

19. Reggie White posted 198 career sacks, which ranks second all-time behind Bruce Smith.

a. True

b. False

20. Which Packers Hall-of-Famer was paid $300 a game and received two $150 checks from different banks to conceal his actual salary?

c. Jim Taylor

d. Bart Starr

e. Don Hutson

f. Ray Nitschke

QUIZ ANSWERS

1. B - LeRoy Butler

2. A - True

3. B - Paul Hornung

4. C - $17 million

5. D - 22

6. A - True

7. B - Travis Jervey & LeShon Johnson

8. B - Phil Bengston

9. C - 90 yards

10. A - True

11. B - Mike Sherman

12. A - Cheeseheads

13. C - Cliff Harris

14. B - False

15. A - 29

16. D - Earl "Curly" Lambeau

17. C - Chicago Bears and Philadelphia Eagles

18. D - Lambeau Leap

19. A - True

20. C - Don Hutson

DID YOU KNOW?

1. Willie Wood was a collegiate quarterback who signed with the Packers as an undrafted free agent. He switched to defensive back in his rookie season and was an All-NFL selection for nine consecutive seasons, from 1962 to 1970. He set an NFL record for most consecutive starts by a safety and was inducted into the Pro Football Hall of Fame in 1989.

2. Clark Hinkle was a Hall of Fame fullback who was also an excellent placekicker and known as the best punter in the NFL. He led the league in field goals twice and averaged 44.5 yards as a punter in 1941.

3. Reggie White was a professional wrestling fan who participated in live events for both World Wrestling Entertainment and World Class Wrestling promotions. He made an appearance at WrestleMania XI in 1995 and had a wrestling match at Slamboree in 1997 against former NFL player Steve McMichael.

4. Hall of Fame quarterback Brett Favre spent 46 days in a drug rehab facility in 1996 after developing an addiction to prescription painkillers. His treatment was mandated by the league office, which threatened Favre with a hefty $900,000 fine if he refused to seek treatment for his addiction.

5. Mason Crosby had a rough start to the 2018 season for the

Packers. He missed a potential game-winning field goal against the Minnesota Vikings in a Week 2 contest that eventually ended in a tie. Three weeks later, he made only one field goal in five attempts and missed an extra point to become the fifth player in NFL history to miss more than four field goals and an extra point in the same game.

6. Eddie Lacy became the first Packer in 42 years to win Offensive Rookie of the Year honors in 2013. He finished the season with 1,178 yards and 11 touchdowns. The following season, he suffered a concussion during the season opener despite wearing the new Speed Flex helmet by Riddell, which claimed the helmets were safer than other models.

7. Datone Jones came up big during the postseason in his second NFL season with the Packers to help the team advance to the NFC Championship game. He became the first player in franchise history to recover a fumble and block a field goal in the same playoff game in a win over the Dallas Cowboys.

8. Morgan Burnett was a steady force in the Packers defensive secondary for several years. He joined James Laurinaitis of the St. Louis Rams as the only two defensive players in the NFL to play every snap in every game during the 2012 season.

9. Brad Jones was a seventh-round draft pick who was thrust into action in his rookie year due to injuries. A savvy player with great instincts and marginal talent, he is also

known for putting a hard hit on a 15-year-old boy who ran onto the field during the 2012 regular-season finale against the Detroit Lions.

10. Jermichael Finley was an electric tight end whose career was cut short due to a spinal injury. The University of Texas product set a then-franchise record with 6 catches for 159 yards in a playoff matchup against the Arizona Cardinals. A helmet-to-helmet hit in 2013 left him paralyzed with little feeling in his legs, but he started gradually recovering the following day.

CHAPTER 9:

NICKNAMES

QUIZ TIME!

1. Which Green Bay Packers legend was nicknamed the "Minister of Defense"?

    a. Ray Nitschke

    b. Lionel Aldridge

    c. Reggie White

    d. John Martinkovic

2. Vince Lombardi's assistant coaches called him "The Mad Scientist."

    a. True

    b. False

3. Chuck Cecil was a hard-hitting defensive back who often left his feet and led with his helmet when making a tackle. What nickname did he get for his reckless style of play?

    a. Scud

    b. Arrow

c. Bullet

d. Missile

4. What legendary Packer was nicknamed "The Gray Ghost of Gonzaga"?

a. Jim Taylor

b. Barty Smith

c. Tony Canadeo

d. Paul Ott Carruth

5. Don Hutson was the first star receiver in NFL history. What was his nickname?

a. The Flash

b. Great Gazelle

c. The Roadrunner

d. Alabama Antelope

6. Packers running back James Starks was nicknamed "Neo" because he wore flashy clothes.

a. True

b. False

7. Which of the following players was called "Golden Boy" because he attended Notre Dame and had blonde hair?

a. Fred Cone

b. Paul Hornung

c. Howie Ferguson

d. Don McIlhenny

8. Legendary Packer Jerry Kramer called his ultra-talented teammate and roommate "Dr. Feelgood." What was the name of his teammate?

a. Ab Wimberly

b. Ezra Johnson

c. Willie Davis

d. Sweeny Williams

9. What three-time Pro Bowl Packers wide receiver was nicknamed "Double-D"?

a. Donald Driver

b. Boyd Dowler

c. Don McIlhenny

d. Dick O'Donnell

10. Gilbert Brown was called "The Gravedigger" in honor of his celebratory dance following a clutch tackle.

a. True

b. False

11. Which of the following running back duos were called "Thunder and Lightning" by Packers fans due to their power and agility?

a. Fred Cone & Tony Canadeo

b. Johnny Blood & Arnie Herber

c. Jim Taylor & Paul Hornung

d. Verne Lewellen & Eddie Kotal

12. To make extra money, Johnny "Blood" McNally needed a fake last name to play semipro football to protect his college eligibility. Where did he see his fake name?

a. Billboard

b. Theater marquee

c. Newspaper ad

d. Train station

13. What nickname was given to Packers linebackers Preston Smith and Za'Darius Smith?

    a. Smith & Co.

    b. Smithereens

    c. Smith Connection

    d. Smith Brothers

14. Ha'Sean Clinton-Dix was given the nickname "Ha Ha" as a young child by his grandmother.

    a. True

    b. False

15. Which Packer started playing linebacker in college before switching to running back as a junior, and was known as "The Truck" in college?

    a. Elijah Pitts

    b. Gerry Ellis

    c. MacArthur Lane

    d. John Brockington

16. What nickname did defensive tackle B.J. Raji give himself after being used as an additional fullback in the Packers' goal-line offense?

    a. The Ice Box

    b. The Freezer

    c. The Dryer

    d. The Water Heater

17. Jordy Nelson caught 69 career touchdown passes in Green Bay and made the Pro Bowl in 2014. What was his nickname?

   a. Mr. Packer
   b. Human Safety Blanket
   c. Slot Machine
   d. White Lightning

18. Because of his tall and thin frame, Ted Hendricks was given a nickname in college that followed him to the NFL. What was he called?

   a. The Mad Stork
   b. Spiderman
   c. Tarantula
   d. Praying Mantis

19. Hall of Fame quarterback Brett Favre was a prolific passer who was known as the "Gunslinger."

   a. True
   b. False

20. Don Majkowski held the single-season record for most games passing for 300 or more yards until Brett Favre broke the record in 1995. What was Majkowski's nickname?

   c. The Majik Man
   d. Maniac
   e. Major
   f. Mowski

QUIZ ANSWERS

1. C - Reggie White

2. B - False

3. A - Scud

4. C - Tony Canadeo

5. D - Alabama Antelope

6. B - False

7. B - Paul Hornung

8. C - Willie Davis

9. A - Donald Driver

10. A - True

11. C - Jim Taylor & Paul Hornung

12. B - Theater Marquee

13. D - Smith Brothers

14. A - True

15. C - MacArthur Lane

16. B - The Freezer

17. D – White Lightning

18. A - The Stork

19. A - True

20. A – Magic

DID YOU KNOW?

1. Mike Michalske was a rugged guard and fullback for the Packers who was called "Iron Mike" by his teammates. A Pro Football Hall-of-Famer, he was a member of the NFL 1920s All-Decade Team. He won three consecutive NFL titles with Green Bay from 1929 to 1931.

2. Emlen Tunnell, who played for the Packers from 1959 through 1961, was the first African-American player to suit up for the New York Giants and also the first African-American to be inducted into the Pro Football Hall of Fame. He was known as "The Gremlin." Tunnell served four years in the United States Coast Guard and was awarded the Silver Lifesaving Medal for heroism for twice rescuing shipmates.

3. Cal Hubbard is the only person who has been inducted into the Pro Football Hall of Fame, College Football Hall of Fame and the Baseball Hall of Fame. He was called the "Big Umpire" because he worked as a professional baseball umpire for the American League.

4. Boob Darling played five years for the Packers and his older brother Lon Darling founded the National Basketball League. His nickname was given to him by his younger sister who called him "booboo," which was later shortened to "boob."

5. Paul "Tiny" Engebretsen played eight seasons on the

Green Bay offensive line and is a member of the Packers Hall of Fame. He was a good placekicker who led the NFL with 10 extra points during his rookie year in 1932 with the Chicago Bears. He also connected for a league-high 18 extra points in 1939 and finished his pro football career with 15 field goals and 54 extra points.

6. Dick Himes was an offensive lineman who was nicknamed "Ox" by his teammates. He wore No. 72 for 10 consecutive seasons and was one of the picketing Packers players who were arrested outside Lambeau Field during the 1974 players' strike.

7. Mike "Scooter" McGruder played one season with the Green Bay Packers during his eight-year NFL career. He was a finalist for the 1997 Bart Starr Award, which is given to the player who best exemplifies outstanding character and leadership.

8. Steve "Mongo" McMichael, who played for the Packers in 1994 after 13 seasons with the Bears, was one of the NFL's top pass rushers. He finished his career with 95 sacks. The University of Texas All-American became a wrestling personality after he retired from football and is a former WCW United States Champion.

9. Keith Jackson was a dynamic tight end for the University of Oklahoma who was nicknamed "Boomer Sooner." During his four-year collegiate career, the Sooners won 42 of 48 games with five losses and one tie. He caught a 71-yard touchdown in the 1986 Orange Bowl to help Oklahoma

defeat Penn State for the national championship. He played on the Packers' 1996 Super Bowl-winning team.

10. Green Bay Packers wide receiver Donald Driver was nicknamed the "Quickie" by his father because he was adept at learning things quickly. He has also published four children's books with the main character named Quickie.

CHAPTER 10:

ALMA MATERS

QUIZ TIME!

1. Who was the defensive end from the University of North Carolina who set a Packers rookie record – since broken – with eight sacks in 1998?

   a. Gabe Wilkins
   b. Keith McKenzie
   c. Jonathan Brown
   d. Vonnie Holliday

2. Packers quarterback Joe Shield attended tiny Trinity College, which is the second-oldest college in Connecticut.

   a. True
   b. False

3. Packers wide receiver Jeff Query was the first NFL player to be drafted out of which school?

   a. Elmhurst College
   b. Millikin University
   c. North Park University
   d. University of Wisconsin-Eau Claire

4. What is the name of the Packers quarterback who played college football at Furman University?

    a. B.J. Coleman
    b. Scott Hunter
    c. David Whitehurst
    d. Anthony Dilweg

5. At which one of the following schools did Packers wide receiver Jeff Janis set a team record of 4,305 receiving yards?

    a. Weber State
    b. Paul Quinn College
    c. Bethel University
    d. Saginaw Valley St.

6. Sterling Sharpe was the first player to have his jersey number retired by South Carolina while still playing for the Gamecocks.

    a. True
    b. False

7. Packers linebacker Bryce Paup attended the University of Northern Iowa. What is the name of the school mascot?

    a. Panthers
    b. Cardinals
    c. Stallions
    d. Jack Rabbits

8. What is the name of the small school that Packers defensive end Gabe Wilkins led to the 1992 NAIA Football Championship game?

a. Radford University

b. Cameron University

c. Gardner–Webb University

d. Tarleton State University

9. Besides Aaron Rodgers, what is the name of another California Bears quarterback who is starting in the NFL?

a. Matt Ryan

b. Drew Lock

c. Josh Allen

d. Jared Goff

10. Green Bay's 2001 first-round pick Jamal Reynolds was a unanimous first-team All-American at Florida State University.

a. True

b. False

11. Packers defensive end Ezra Johnson attended a historically black liberal arts college, which lost its accreditation in 2003 and no longer has a football program. What is the name of the school?

a. Miles College

b. Morris Brown College

c. LeMoyne–Owen College

d. Kentucky State University

12. Who was the Texas Tech running back that the Packers took in the first round of the 1965 NFL Draft?

a. Perry Williams

b. Junior Coffey

c. Donny Anderson

d. Jim Grabowski

13. Packers wide receiver Donald Driver was a decorated track star at Alcorn State. What sport did he qualify for at the 1996 Olympic Field Trials?

a. Long jump

b. 100-meter dash

c. 200-meter hurdles

d. High jump

14. Former San Diego State defensive end Kabeer Gbaja-Biamila finished his college career with a school-record 33 sacks. He has 74.5 sacks in nine seasons with the Packers.

a. True

b. False

15. Who was the Packers quarterback who led the Rice Owls to the 1949 Southwest Conference championship?

a. Arnie Galiffa

b. Tobin Rote

c. Stan Heath

d. Ernie Case

16. What Packer Hall-of-Famer attended Gonzaga University?

a. Jim Ringo

b. Jerry Kramer

c. Tony Canadeo

d. Dave Robinson

17. Who was the first quarterback from the University of California to be drafted by the Packers?

    a. Babe Parilli
    b. Aaron Rodgers
    c. Brian Brohm
    d. Rich Campbell

18. The Packers selected Richmond running back Barty Smith with a first-round pick in 1974 but their fourth-round draft choice Don Woods, chosen 122 picks later, had a more productive NFL career. What school did Woods attend?

    a. UTEP
    b. New Mexico
    c. Idaho State
    d. Wyoming

19. Ball State defensive end Keith McKenzie, the Packers' 252nd pick in 1996, posted 29.5 sacks and one interception in 95 NFL games.

    a. True
    b. False

20. What Packers defensive back played college football at Bethune-Cookman and had his career end prematurely due to a neck injury?

    a. Pat Lee
    b. Joey Thomas
    c. Nick Collins
    d. Jerron McMillian

QUIZ ANSWERS

1. D - Vonnie Holliday

2. A - True

3. B – Millikin University

4. C - David Whitehurst

5. D - Saginaw Valley St.

6. B - False

7. A - Panthers

8. C - Gardner–Webb University

9. D - Jared Goff

10. A - True

11. B - Morris Brown College

12. C - Donny Anderson

13. D - High jump

14. A - True

15. B - Tobin Rote

16. C - Tony Canadeo

17. D - Rich Campbell

18. B - New Mexico

19. A - True

20. C - Nick Collins

DID YOU KNOW?

1. The great Packers guard Jerry Kramer was a productive two-way player for the University of Idaho, and also lettered in track and field. He played in the College All-Star Game and was a member of the team that beat the reigning NFL champion Detroit Lions. The Vandals retired his No. 64 on his 27th birthday in 1963.

2. Ray Nitschke, long-time Packers middle linebacker, was a terrible college student who was known to have an attitude problem. His dream of playing quarterback in the Rose Bowl was dashed when he was switched to fullback and linebacker. He never wore a face mask and had four of his front teeth knocked out in a game against Ohio State in 1956.

3. Clarke Hinkle, who was named first-team All-Pro fullback four times in his ten seasons with the Packers, was a standout offensive talent at Bucknell University who scored eight touchdowns in a Thanksgiving Day matchup against Dickinson in 1929. He scored an incredible 37 touchdowns during his college career and led the Bisons to a perfect season in his final year in 1931. He was elected to the College Football Hall of Fame in 1971.

4. P.J. Pope finished his collegiate career as one of the most prolific running backs in the history of Bowling Green State University. He was the first player to tally 3,000

rushing yards and 1,000 receiving yards for the school and is the program's fourth all-time leading rusher. Pope played briefly for the Packers in 2006.

5. Brandon Saine was a versatile running back at Ohio State who signed with the Packers as an undrafted free agent. He was a speedster who posted an unofficial time of 4.25 seconds in the 40-yard dash. During his first season with the Buckeyes, he established himself as a rusher, a receiver and a blocker.

6. Vai Sikahema was the first person born in Tonga to play in the NFL. He was a running back and return specialist at Brigham Young University, and he returned a punt for a touchdown during his first season with the Cougars. He was a member of the 1984 Brigham Young squad that claimed the national championship with an undefeated 13-0 record. He spent eight seasons in the NFL as a punt and kick returner, including one season with the Packers.

7. Barty Smith spent seven seasons with the Packers, mostly as a reserve fullback, after leading the University of Richmond Spiders to the Southern Conference championship and was a two-time All-Southern Conference selection. He finished his college career ranked eighth on the school's all-time rushing list with 1,941 yards and was named MVP of the 1973 East-West Shrine Game. In 1976, he was elected to the University of Richmond Athletic Hall of Fame.

8. Maurice Smith was a first-team All-MEAC running back who starred at North Carolina A&T State University. He

signed with the Packers as an undrafted free agent in 2000 and received the highest signing bonus of all undrafted signees after negotiating his own contract.

9. Jordy Nelson began his college career as a walk-on defensive back at Kansas State University. He was switched to wide receiver during his freshman season and was one of the nation's most productive college receivers in his senior year, when he was a consensus All-American and Biletnikoff Award finalist after recording 122 receptions for 1,606 yards and 11 touchdowns. In his nine seasons with the Packers, he caught 550 passes for 7,848 yards and 69 TDs.

10. Greg Jennings was twice selected for the Pro Bowl during his seven seasons with the Packers. His college career at Western Michigan University got off to a slow start because of a broken ankle during his freshman season. However, he blossomed into one of the top wide receivers in the history of the Mid-American Conference, with 172 catches over his final two seasons for 2,351 yards and 25 touchdowns.

CHAPTER 11:

IN THE DRAFT ROOM

QUIZ TIME!

1. The Packers drafted UTEP running back Aaron Jones in the fifth round of the 2017 NFL Draft. What country has Jones resided in besides the United States?

   a. Italy
   b. Canada
   c. Germany
   d. Philippines

2. Green Bay's 2016 third-round pick, Blake Martinez, signed a three-year, $30 million free-agent contract with the New York Giants after four seasons in Green Bay.

   a. True
   b. False

3. The Packers drafted Penn State defensive end Bruce Clark with the fourth pick overall in the 1980 draft, but he chose to play in the Canadian Football League. What Canadian team did he play for?

a. Calgary Stampeders

b. Montreal Alouettes

c. Edmonton Eskimos

d. Toronto Argonauts

4. Who was the Green Bay Packers' very first draft choice?

a. Russ Letlow

b. Theron Ward

c. J.W. Wheeler

d. Ed Jankowski

5. The Packers had two first-round selections in the 2019 NFL Draft. Which two players did Green Bay take with the 12th and 21st picks?

a. Kevin King & Josh Jones

b. Rashan Gary & Darnell Savage

c. Kenny Clark & Jason Spriggs

d. Jaire Alexander & Josh Jackson

6. Babe Parilli was known as "Gold Finger" because he was one of the best holders in the history of football.

a. True

b. False

7. What is the name of the serial killer drafted by the Packers in 1974?

a. Doug Troszak

b. Harold Holton

c. Emanuel Armstrong

d. Randy Woodfield

8. The Packers drafted University of California quarterback Rich Campbell with the sixth pick overall in the 1981 NFL Draft. What was his profession after his football career ended?

   a. Truck driver
   b. Fitness trainer
   c. Newspaper columnist
   d. Funeral director

9. What is the name of the Packers' 15th-round draft pick who became an NFL head coach?

   a. Dan Reeves
   b. Dave Wannstedt
   c. Dennis Green
   d. Ted Marchibroda

10. Green Bay's 2020 first-round pick Jordan Love threw five touchdown passes and was named the MVP of the 2018 Sugar Bowl.

    a. True
    b. False

11. Which Packers Hall-of-Famer was selected with the 80th pick of the NFL draft?

    a. Jim Ringo
    b. Ray Nitschke
    c. Jerry Kramer
    d. Tony Canadeo

12. Forrest Gregg was drafted in the second round by the

Packers in 1956 and later served as a head coach in the NFL. How many teams did he coach?

a. 1
b. 2
c. 3
d. 4

13. The Packers selected wide receiver Phil Epps with the 321st pick in the 1982 NFL Draft. How many career catches did this late-round selection have?

a. 103
b. 175
c. 200
d. 244

14. Louisville running back Ernie Green was drafted in the 14th round by the Packers in 1962 but was traded to the Cleveland Browns during training camp.

a. True
b. False

15. In the 1963 NFL Draft, the two-time defending NFL champion Green Bay Packers selected a quarterback from Notre Dame in the 12th round. However, he opted to sign with the AFL's Buffalo Bills. What was his name?

a. Val Keckin
b. Dave Bennett
c. Gale Weidner
d. Daryle Lamonica

16. What did the media call the 61-yard Hail Mary touchdown pass that 2014 third-rounder Richard Rodgers hauled in to beat the Detroit Lions?

    a. The Motown Miracle
    b. The Motor City Miracle
    c. The Miracle in Motown
    d. The Detroit Miracle

17. Which of the Packers' fifth-round draft picks averaged a league-high 5.5 yards per carry during his first two seasons in the NFL?

    a. Dorsey Levens
    b. Aaron Jones
    c. Travis Jervey
    d. De'Mond Parker

18. Who was the Hall of Fame defensive back the Packers drafted in the third round of the 1952 NFL Draft?

    a. Bobby Dillon
    b. Bill Roffler
    c. Rip Collins
    d. Rebel Steiner

19. Brent Fullwood, who was drafted by the Packers with the fourth overall pick, was the first of four Auburn running backs to get selected in the 1987 NFL Draft.

    a. True
    b. False

20. How many wide receivers were chosen in the 2014 NFL

Draft before Green Bay selected Davante Adams with the 53rd pick?

a. 5
b. 6
c. 7
d. 8

QUIZ ANSWERS

1. C - Germany

2. A - True

3. D - Toronto Argonauts

4. A - Russ Letlow

5. B - Rashan Gary & Darnell Savage

6. A - True

7. D - Randy Woodfield

8. C - Newspaper columnist

9. B - Dave Wannstedt

10. B - False

11. A - Jim Ringo

12. C - 3

13. C - 200

14. A - True

15. D - Daryle Lamonica

16. C - The Miracle in Motown

17. B - Aaron Jones

18. A - Bobby Dillon

19. A - True

20. D – 8

DID YOU KNOW?

1. Aaron Rodgers' draft-day slide to the 24th pick was ranked No. 1 on the NFL Network's Top 10 Draft Day Moments. The former California Golden Bears standout is one of six quarterbacks — the others are Akili Smith, Joey Harrington, Trent Dilfer, Kyle Boller and David Carr — who were coached by Jeff Tedford and selected in the first round of an NFL draft.

2. Nick Barnett was the 29th overall pick of the Packers in the 2003 NFL Draft. The Oregon State product was the third linebacker selected behind Terrell Suggs and Calvin Pace. He signed a $6 million contract that included a $3.21 million signing bonus and was named the starting middle linebacker during training camp.

3. Javon Walker was an athletic freak who was the 20th overall pick in the 2002 NFL Draft. Before transferring to Florida State University, he saw action at Jones County Junior College and was a teammate of future NFL wide receiver Deion Branch. During his rookie year with the Packers, he became the fourth player in league history to post 100 receiving yards in each of his first two playoff games.

4. Jamal Reynolds was an All-American defensive end at Florida State University who played only three seasons in the NFL. He posted 58 tackles and 12 sacks during his

senior year and was the 10th overall pick in the 2001 NFL draft. He finished his disappointing pro football career with only three sacks in 18 games with the Packers.

5. Bubba Franks, who spent eight seasons with the Packers, was the 14th overall pick in the 2000 NFL Draft. Blessed with soft hands and uncanny speed and agility for a 6-foot-6, 265-pound body frame, he set a University of Miami record for most touchdowns by a tight end.

6. Antuan Edwards was an All-American safety at Clemson University who was selected by the Packers with the 25th overall pick in the 1999 NFL Draft. He started 33 games for the Tigers and finished his college career with eight interceptions and 219 tackles. Edwards had 7 interceptions in 53 games with the Packers.

7. Although Penn State defensive end Bruce Clark was drafted fourth overall by the Packers in the 1980 NFL Draft, the All-American opted to sign with the Toronto Argonauts of the Canadian Football League. In 1978, he became the first junior to win the Lombardi Award, which is given to the best college defensive lineman in the country.

8. Barry Smith was selected by the Packers with the 21st overall pick in the 1973 NFL Draft. The Florida State wide receiver played three seasons with Green Bay before finishing his four-year NFL career with the Tampa Bay Buccaneers.

9. The Packers selected Ohio State running back John

Brockington with the ninth overall pick in the 1971 NFL Draft. He was the 1971 NFL Offensive Rookie of the Year and became the first NFL player to rush for 1,000 or more yards in each of his first three seasons. He was selected to three straight Pro Bowl teams from 1971 to 1973.

10. Notre Dame defensive tackle Mike McCoy was an All-American who was drafted by the Packers with the second overall pick in the 1970 NFL Draft. He finished sixth in the Heisman Trophy balloting in his senior year and was the Associated Press Lineman of the Year. He led Green Bay in sacks twice and was named the Packers Rookie of the Year in 1970.

CHAPTER 12:

THE TRADING POST

QUIZ TIME!

1. Which one of the following players did the Packers acquire from Los Angeles in 1974 for two first-round draft picks, two second-rounders and a third-rounder?

   a. Tony Baker
   b. John Hadl
   c. Larry Brooks
   d. Jack Reynolds

2. 2. A five-time Pro Bowl selection for the Packers, fullback Jim Taylor rushed for a career-high 874 yards and 10 touchdowns after being traded to the New Orleans Saints.

   a. True
   b. False

3. Which former first-round draft pick did the Packers trade to Cleveland in exchange for quarterback DeShone Kizer?

   a. Kenny Clark
   b. Nick Perry

    c. Ha Ha Clinton-Dix

    d. Damarious Randall

4. What team traded for Packers Hall of Fame defensive back Herb Adderley before the start of the 1970 regular season?

    a. Detroit Lions

    b. Chicago Bears

    c. Dallas Cowboys

    d. Kansas City Chiefs

5. The Packers traded Brett Favre to the New York Jets in 2008, but which of the following teams had also negotiated with Green Bay to acquire Favre?

    a. Arizona Cardinals

    b. Tampa Bay Buccaneers

    c. Minnesota Vikings

    d. Miami Dolphins

6. After being traded to the Chargers in 1979, Packers cornerback Willie Buchanon played four more seasons in the NFL.

    a. True

    b. False

7. Hall of Fame receiver James Lofton was traded to the Los Angeles Raiders after nine seasons with Green Bay. How many other teams did Lofton play for after being traded by the Packers?

    a. 1

    b. 2

c. 3

d. 4

8. Which player spent two years as Brett Favre's backup before he was traded to the Seattle Seahawks to begin his career as a starting quarterback?

   a. Mike Tomczak

   b. Anthony Dilweg

   c. Don Majkowski

   d. Matt Hasselbeck

9. In 2008, Green Bay traded their 30th pick to the New York Jets for the 36th and 113th picks. Who did the Packers select with the 36th pick?

   a. Matt Flynn

   b. Jordy Nelson

   c. Jeremy Thompson

   d. Jermichael Finley

10. The Green Bay Packers traded safety Ha Ha Clinton-Dix to the Washington Redskins for a 2019 4th-round pick.

    a. True

    b. False

11. Which of the following quarterbacks did the Packers select in 2008 with the second-round draft pick obtained from the Cleveland Browns in exchange for defensive tackle Corey Williams?

    a. Erik Ainge

    b. Chad Henne

c. Brian Brohm

d. Josh Johnson

12. The Packers traded the 41st, 73rd and 83rd picks in the 2009 NFL Draft to the New England Patriots for the 26th and 162nd picks. Who did Green Bay select with the 26th pick?

a. Jarius Wynn

b. Jamon Meredith

c. Quinn Johnson

d. Clay Matthews

13. Because of a contract dispute, Green Bay traded a disgruntled cornerback and a future draft choice to the New Orleans Saints in exchange for third-string quarterback J.T. O'Sullivan and a second-round draft pick. What was the name of the player that was sent to the Saints?

a. Micah Hyde

b. Mike McKenzie

c. Aaron Rouse

d. Ha Ha Clinton-Dix

14. The Baltimore Ravens sent a 2020 seventh-round pick to the Packers in exchange for running back Ty Montgomery.

a. True

b. False

15. The Packers traded two picks to the Philadelphia Eagles in the 2010 NFL Draft for the 71st pick in order to draft which one of the following players?

a. Brian Bulaga
b. T.J. Lang
c. Morgan Burnett
d. Marshall Newhouse

16. How many draft picks did Green Bay send to the Indianapolis Colts in the 2016 NFL Draft for a second-round pick to select offensive tackle Jason Spriggs?

a. 1
b. 2
c. 3
d. 4

17. In the 2018 NFL Draft, the Packers moved up nine spots by trading the 27th, 76th and 186th picks to the Seattle Seahawks for the 18th and 248th picks. What player did the Packers draft with that 18th pick?

a. Jaire Alexander
b. Rashan Gary
c. Kevin King
d. Montravius Adams

18. The Packers sign an undrafted free agent in 2017 and eventually traded him to the Indianapolis Colts for linebacker Antonio Morrison. Who was he?

a. David Rivers
b. David Talley
c. Raysean Pringle
d. Lenzy Pipkins

19. To move up four spots in the 2020 NFL Draft to select quarterback Jordan Love with the 26th pick, the Packers sent the Miami Dolphins their first- and second-round selections.

    a. True
    b. False

20. Green Bay traded out of the first round of the 2017 NFL Draft to allow the Cleveland Browns to draft tight end David Njoku. Who was the player the Packers selected with the first pick of the second round?

    a. Oren Burks
    b. Josh Jones
    c. Kevin King
    d. Cole Madison

QUIZ ANSWERS

1. B - John Hadl

2. B - False

3. D - Damarious Randall

4. C - Dallas Cowboys

5. B - Tampa Bay Buccaneers

6. A - True

7. D - 4

8. D - Matt Hasselbeck

9. B - Jordy Nelson

10. A - True

11. C - Brian Brohm

12. D - Clay Matthews

13. B - Mike McKenzie

14. A - True

15. C - Morgan Burnett

16. C - 3

17. A - Jaire Alexander

18. D - Lenzy Pipkins

19. B - False

20. C - Kevin King

DID YOU KNOW?

1. The Packers traded former All-Pro center Jim Ringo to the Philadelphia Eagles in 1964, but the details of the trade have been mired in controversy for decades. Although it is widely believed that Lombardi had been working on a deal with the Eagles, Jerry Kramer wrote a different story in his memoir. He alleged that Ringo and his agent visited Lombardi to negotiate a new contract, which angered Lombardi so much he left the room for five minutes and returned to announce that Ringo had just been traded to Philadelphia.

2. The Packers acquired future Hall of Fame quarterback Brett Favre from the Atlanta Falcons for a first-round pick in 1992. The Falcons used the 19th overall pick from Green Bay to select running back Tony Smith, who played with Favre at Southern Mississippi. While Favre went on to rewrite the NFL record books, Smith played only three NFL seasons, compiling 329 career rushing yards and two touchdowns.

3. The Packers dealt fullback Earl Gros to the Philadelphia Eagles in exchange for linebacker Lee Roy Caffey and a first-round draft pick. Green Bay used that pick to draft halfback-punter Donny Anderson with the seventh overall selection in the 1965 NFL Draft.

4. Green Bay traded future Pro Football Hall of Fame

defensive back Herb Adderley to the Dallas Cowboys in 1970. Adderley had a poor relationship with Packers head coach Phil Bengtson, who he felt kept him off the Pro Bowl team in 1969. Adderley requested a trade instead of reporting to the Packers training camp.

5. The Packers acquired defensive lineman John Martinkovic from the Washington Redskins during training camp in 1951. Green Bay sent end Ted Cook to the Redskins, but he had retired the previous July. Martinkovic was selected to three straight Pro Bowls from 1953 to 1955.

6. Green Bay traded three players, Elijah Pitts, Lee Roy Caffey and Bob Hyland, to the Chicago Bears for the second overall pick in the 1970 NFL Draft. The Packers used the draft pick to select Notre Dame defensive tackle Mike McCoy, who led the team in sacks on two different occasions.

7. The Packers traded former first-rounder Damarious Randall to the Cleveland Browns in 2018 for backup quarterback DeShone Kizer and swapped a pair of middle-round draft picks as well. Randall played two seasons with the Browns before signing a one-year contract with the Las Vegas Raiders in 2020. Kizer spent a lone season with the Packers and Raiders and was a free agent heading into the 2020 regular season.

8. Cornerback Willie Buchanon overcame a broken leg twice en route to a successful NFL career. He intercepted four passes in a 1978 game against the San Diego Chargers and

led the NFC with nine picks that year. He was traded to the Chargers the following season for draft picks in the first and seventh rounds.

9. The Packers traded future Hall of Fame wide receiver James Lofton to the Oakland Raiders in 1987 for two undisclosed draft picks. Lofton was awaiting trial on a sexual assault charge and Green Bay opted to trade the talented receiver. Green Bay received a third-round pick in the 1987 NFL Draft and a 1988 conditional fourth-round pick. Lofton went on to play seven more seasons in the NFL with four different teams.

10. The Packers shipped running back Ty Montgomery to the Baltimore Ravens a mere two days after Montgomery fumbled a kickoff return in a heartbreaking loss to the Los Angeles Rams. The Ravens sent Green Bay a seventh-round pick in the 2020 NFL Draft.

CHAPTER 13:

SUPER BOWL SPECIAL

QUIZ TIME!

1. Which Green Bay safety intercepted a pass in Super Bowl I that helped the Packers erupt for 21 unanswered points en route to a blowout win?

   a. Doug Hart
   b. Tom Brown
   c. Willie Wood
   d. Hank Gremminger

2. 2. Green Bay quarterback Bart Starr was named MVP of Super Bowl I and Super Bowl II.

   a. True
   b. False

3. The Packers beat the New England Patriots 35-21 in Super Bowl XXXI. All the players in that game wore a special helmet decal to pay tribute to a former NFL commissioner who had recently died. What was the name of the commissioner?

a. Austin Gunsel

b. Pete Rozelle

c. Elmer Layden

d. Paul Tagliabue

4. Super Bowl XLV was the first Super Bowl without cheerleaders since Green Bay and Pittsburgh were two of the six teams that did not have cheerleaders in 2010. Which of the following teams DID have cheerleaders that season?

a. Chicago Bears

b. Detroit Lions

c. New York Giants

d. Oakland Raiders

5. Green Bay racked up four interceptions and five sacks in Super Bowl XXXI to defeat the Patriots. Which Packers defensive end set a Super Bowl record with three sacks?

a. Sean Jones

b. Robert Brown

c. Reggie White

d. Vonnie Holliday

6. Super Bowl I was the only NFL championship game that was simulcast in the United States on ABC, NBC and CBS.

a. True

b. False

7. Packers defensive back Herb Adderley had the first pick-six in Super Bowl history in Green Bay's win over the

Raiders in Super Bowl II. How long was his interception return for a touchdown?

   c. 45 yards
   d. 60 yards
   e. 72 yards
   f. 80 yards

8. The Packers outlasted the New England Patriots to win Super Bowl XXXI. Who was named Super Bowl MVP?

   a. Desmond Howard
   b. Brett Favre
   c. Antonio Freeman
   d. Keith Jackson

9. Which Green Bay lineman became the youngest player in Super Bowl history to start in the big game at the age of 21 years and 322 days old?

   a. T.J. Lang
   b. Scott Wells
   c. Josh Sitton
   d. Bryan Bulaga

10. Super Bowl II was the first title game that the NFL used the Y-shaped goalposts with only one supporting post instead of two.

   a. True
   b. False

11. Which Packer delivered a hit on Pittsburgh quarterback Ben Roethlisberger in Super Bowl XLV that resulted in

Nick Collins intercepting the pass and returning it for a touchdown?

a. B.J. Raji
b. Howard Green
c. Ryan Pickett
d. Clay Matthews

12. Bart Starr threw a 37-yard touchdown pass to give the Packers a 7-0 lead in Super Bowl I. Who was the backup receiver who caught the touchdown pass?

a. Max McGee
b. Ron Kramer
c. Marv Fleming
d. Rich McGeorge

13. Despite winning Super Bowl XLV, the Packers were missing numerous starters heading into the playoffs. How many starters were either suspended or on injured reserve?

a. 5
b. 6
c. 7
d. 8

14. Super Bowl XLV, pitting the Packers against the Steelers, was the second Super Bowl played in the Dallas–Fort Worth area.

a. True
b. False

15. Desmond Howard was voted the Most Valuable Player of Super Bowl XXXI after returning a kickoff for a touchdown. How long was his game-clinching touchdown return?

    a. 90 yards
    b. 95 yards
    c. 96 yards
    d. 99 yards

16. Before being renamed the Vince Lombardi Trophy in 1970, what were the words inscribed on the award?

    a. Professional Football Championship
    b. NFL & AFL Football Championship
    c. National Football League Championship
    d. World Professional Football Championship

17. Which one of the following Packers was named the MVP of Super Bowl XLV?

    a. Jordy Nelson
    b. Hines Ward
    c. Aaron Rodgers
    d. Greg Jennings

18. When Bart Starr was injured in the fourth quarter of Super Bowl II, which Packers backup quarterback replaced him?

    a. John Hadl
    b. Scott Hunter
    c. Lynn Dickey
    d. Zeke Bratkowski

19. The Green Bay Packers defeated the Pittsburgh Steelers in Super Bowl XLV to become the first NFC sixth seed to win a Super Bowl.

    a. True
    b. False

20. With their victory over the Green Bay Packers in Super Bowl XLV, the Green Bay Packers added to their record-setting number of league titles. How many NFL championships have the Packers won?

    a. 10
    b. 11
    c. 12
    d. 13

QUIZ ANSWERS

1. C - Willie Wood

2. A - True

3. B - Pete Rozelle

4. D - Oakland Raiders

5. C - Reggie White

6. B - False

7. B - 60 yards

8. A - Desmond Howard

9. D - Bryan Bulaga

10. A - True

11. B - Howard Green

12. A - Max McGee

13. D - 8

14. B - False

15. D - 99 yards

16. D - World Professional Football Championship

17. C - Aaron Rodgers

18. D - Zeke Bratkowski

19. A - True

20. D – 13

DID YOU KNOW?

1. The Packers routed the AFL's Kansas City Chiefs in Super Bowl I behind a strong performance from reserve receiver Max McGee. Although he caught only four passes during the regular season, McGee caught seven passes for 138 yards and two scores from Super Bowl I MVP Bart Starr. An injured Paul Hornung was the only player on the Green Bay roster who did not play in the game.

2. Green Bay became the second sixth seed to reach the Super Bowl and pulled off the upset win in Super Bowl XLV. Packers quarterback Aaron Rodgers completed 24 of 39 passes for 304 yards and three touchdowns to earn MVP honors. With the win, the Packers won their fourth Super Bowl and 13th overall NFL championship.

3. The Packers hoisted their first Lombardi Trophy in 30 years with an exciting victory over the New England Patriots at Super Bowl XXXI. Return specialist Desmond Howard was chosen as the MVP after setting a then-Super Bowl record with a 99-yard kickoff return for a touchdown.

4. The reigning Super Bowl champion Green Bay Packers were the first team favored to win by double digits to lose a Super Bowl in 28 years. Denver running back Terrell Davis overcame a severe migraine attack to rush for 157 yards and three touchdowns in Super Bowl XXXII to earn the Most Valuable Player award.

5. The Packers captured their second consecutive NFL title with a lopsided victory over the Oakland Raiders in Super Bowl II. Herb Adderley had a 60-yard pick-six and Don Chandler drilled four field goals to help Green Bay pound the AFL champion. Bart Starr was named the Super Bowl MVP for the second straight year.

6. Super Bowl I was a spectacle that featured a flying demonstration by the hydrogen-peroxide-propelled Bell Rocket Air Men. The duo used rocket packs and flew around the stadium. The inaugural Super Bowl is also the only time when the numeric yard markers were five yards apart, rather than 10 yards apart.

7. Packers safety Eugene Robinson foiled Denver's attempt to put Super Bowl XXXII out of reach in the third quarter after the Packers had fumbled the ball on their own 22-yard line. John Elway tried to connect with Rod Smith on a post pattern to the end zone which would have given the Broncos a 31-17 advantage. However, Robinson intercepted the pass to keep the Packers within striking distance.

8. Green Bay used a tenacious defense in the second half to break open a close game against the Kansas City Chiefs in Super Bowl I. Willie Wood picked off an errant Len Dawson pass early in the third quarter to set up a touchdown that gave the Packers a 21-10 lead. The defensive unit came through again two possessions later with a pair of sacks to set up another touchdown that sealed the Packers title-clinching win.

9. Green Bay started Super Bowl XXXII in grand fashion and became only the third team to take the opening kickoff and score a touchdown. Brett Favre connected with Antonio Freeman to give the Packers an early lead. However, Green Bay turned the ball over three times and became the first NFC team in 14 seasons to lose a Super Bowl.

10. Super Bowl XXXI between the Packers and Patriots started with a bang as the two teams set a Super Bowl record with 24 combined points in the opening quarter. However, Brett Favre led Green Bay's offense to 17 points in the second quarter, highlighted by an 81-yard touchdown strike to Antonio Freeman. The win was the 13th consecutive victory for the NFC champion in the title game.

CONCLUSION

The Green Bay Packers have won more NFL championships than any other team in league history. The Packers are the only franchise to win three consecutive NFL titles, and they did it on two different occasions. Green Bay is also the only franchise that is owned by its fans.

Curly Lambeau and George Calhoun founded the team in 1919 and the Packers joined the National Football League in 1921. The Packers' first dynasty began in 1929 when Green Bay won its first league championship before repeating as champion in both 1930 and 1931. The franchise repeated the hat trick from 1965 to 1967 under Hall-of-Fame head coach Vince Lombardi.

The Packers have had some of the best players to ever play the game showcase their talents at historic Lambeau Field. Wide receiver Don Hutson revolutionized the position and is regarded as one of the best pass-catchers to ever play in the NFL. Some of the early players who became Hall-of-Famers are Arnie Herber, Clarke Hinkle, Cal Hubbard, John (Blood) McNally, Mike Michalske and Tony Canadeo.

The 1960's began a new era for the Packers as Lombardi built a team of numerous future Hall-of-Famers like Jim Taylor, Forrest Gregg, Bart Starr, Ray Nitschke, Herb Adderley, Willie Davis, Jim Ringo, Paul Hornung, Willie Wood and Henry Jordan.

Green Bay continued its renaissance in the 1990s into the 21st century with a pair of Super Bowl victories spearheaded by quarterbacks Brett Favre and Aaron Rodgers. This fun-filled trivia book is a tribute to all the men who contributed to the success of the Packers franchise.